A SPLENDID AWAKENING

Kalu Onwuka

𝕲𝕻

Granada Publishing

Los Angeles, California

A Splendid Awakening

Copyright 2014 © Kalu Onwuka

Published in Los Angeles, California by Granada Publishers. Granada Publishers is wholly owned by Granada Publishing Company, Los Angeles, California.

Granada Publishing titles may be purchased in bulk for educational, business, fundraising or sales promotional use. For information please e-mail **sales@granadapublishing.com**.

Library of Congress Cataloging-in-Publication data.

A Splendid Awakening/Kalu Onwuka

LCCN: 2014932729

ISBN: 978-0-9900203-3-2

ISBN: 0990020339

Printed in the United States

Dedication

I will like to dedicate this book *A Splendid Awakening*, which is part of *Poems in Faithfulness to the Divine* series, to all those who have shared the gifts of light and love with me either in formal or informal settings. You are too numerous to count but you have my heart-felt gratitude. I will also like to share the series with all those who love poetry and the everlasting beauty of simple words fitly spoken. Oftentimes in life, the will to act is not so much enabled by what is said but how it is said.

Acknowledgments

As always, I will first like to acknowledge Christ Jesus as the Lord of my life. He is my muse and it is his Spirit that enables me to write. Also, I will like to acknowledge that it is not possible to see through an undertaking such as *Poems in Faithfulness to the Divine* series without the loyal support of family, friends and well-wishers. You have all been there from the conception, writing and the publication process. I will like to acknowledge all your help for you continue to give me cause to hope for the best in mankind. It is such goodness that you share that evokes the pure love and good hope for better extolled within these poems.

CONTENTS

CONTENTS

CONTENTS

CONTENTS

CONTENTS

CONTENTS

OTHER BOOKS BY KALU ONWUKA INCLUDE-

(Poetry)

Anthems in the Glorious Dawn

In Enchantment of Eternity

Tones of the Stellar

The Melody of Light

(Studies for Spirit, Mind and Body)

Nuggets of Resurrection

Pulses of the Divine Heart

Etching for the Faithful Heart

No Hurry to Horeb

(Quotations and Insights)

Capsules of Divine Splendor

All titles are available for purchase through Granada Publishers at **granadapublishing.com.** The author can be contacted through his website at **kaluonwuka.com.**

FOREWORD

This book of poetry titled *A Splendid Awakening* is the fourth volume in the *Poems in Faithfulness to the Divine* series which is a compilation of original poems that speak about places that man must leave behind in order to find the better in life.

There are ninety-two original compelling poems in this volume which explore how man must let go of his old ways of thinking so that he can move beyond his past mistakes into a better future. There are such poems that speak about how the old way of man's thinking leads to envy and strife as well as confine him to a state of little-mindedness, short-sightedness and selfishness. There are other poems that tell that it is possible to transcend the clamor that clouds our lives and be empowered to hear as well as join the conversations in heavenly places in a redeeming light.

A Splendid Awakening is a must-read for persons of faith who love poetry as well as fans of poetry with doubts about faith. To be read on its own or in sequence with the other volumes, it is sure to nourish the mind, heart and soul as well as help readers achieve spiritual transformation.

Kalu Onwuka

Good and Lovely

Wisdom calls all men to hope for the best in life

The uplifting that is lovely and of a good report

And to share the words of truth with the blinded

Where worldliness has precluded the divine light

The noise of the world dampens man's spirit

And fills him with much unbecoming thoughts

Which take shape to drag down his life in dust

For tis his thoughts that become reality for man

The mind that is not cluttered with much wants

Leaves enough room for the important to thrive

For such is cleared of undesirable debris of life

And freed from the cloudiness that inhibits vision

Good and Lovely (Cont'd)

Clarity comes when cloudiness has been cleared

For with good vision much can be clearly seen

So the nature and state of things can be known

And room made for the good and lovely to thrive

The good and lovely count with the precious in life

In a treasure-chest to be held very near and dear

But the bad and undesirable have to be discarded

Into a dust-bin that must be kept far and distant

End

Love Disconnected

Man's sins can be cast into two categories

One does kills the spirit but the other wounds

Such that is dead is left with no reason to hope

But that which is wounded can be rehabilitated

The sins that wound the spirit choke the flow

To make the power of God be of reduced effect

But that which kills the spirit disconnects man

From divine goodness and redemptive power

God prepares and anoints a willing advocate

One full of compassion for men's weaknesses

Such he gives knowledge to help the wounded

Best that heaven offers for plea of repentance

Love Disconnected (Cont'd)

There is always hope for man thru repentance

But nothing for the man who has rejected truth

Except darkness that cuts off from the divine will

To leave him powerless to fight spiritual battles

Such that's disconnected is one without purpose

That expends much energy after the fruitless

Much like one trapped in a ditch and helpless

Who searches for an escape but never finds it

End

Record of the Faithful

The good gifts of the Divine are obtained

By obedience to God's law and commands

He that is faithful is led by hand of Destiny

Into the heart of Providence soon enough

Tis thru obedience that man is affirmed

And the spirit of life comes to dwell in him

So he will come into that certain wisdom

Where heaven can trust and count on him

Heaven dutifully watches and records all

Everything that humankind does on earth

All are called to moderation and sobriety

For by deeds and actions are men judged

Record of the Faithful (Cont'd)

Those who yield to the divine guiding hand

Are molded into vessels worthy of honor

By the Master craftsman who's without par

And blesses mankind with the best in love

Faithfulness asks man to live a certain way

So that the record of his activities on earth

Is deemed to be worthy up where it counts

In heaven where all men's deeds are known

Such handiworks of the faithful should be

A fitting composite to testify about true love

And the worthiness of truth framed in light

In template that defines the mold of mercy

End

A Safe Margin

God always makes a way available

Thru the medium of the Holy Ghost

A sort of feedback medium in place

To keep man safe and well-informed

There is a path laid for the righteous

A safe margin within the will of God

On which the faithful must walk along

And never stray too far or wide from

By a voice that whispers to his soul

The spirit in man makes him aware

Thru convictions 'bout the wages of sin

To keep him within Life's safe margin

A Safe Margin (Cont'd)

The faithful that stays within the fold

Will be guarded by the Father's love

For beyond the safe margin appointed

Lurks much danger for the unwary soul

Tis a dreadful zone where death roams

And the spirit of life cares not for much

Tis a region where angels fear to tread

A bad-land to be avoided by all means

End

The Holy Ghost Perfects

The perfecting process is not rushed

Tis a custom fitting process of sorts

Much like the purification of gold

With no mark to define perfection

Journey of spiritual transformation

Continues with an everlasting hope

But there is a threshold to be met

Before man's joined with the divine

The gift of the Holy Ghost is given

Thru increasing and growing faith

So man can have due information

And insightful knowledge in his aid

He helps the faithful to avoid pitfalls

Correct and change course in time

Also to deal better and manage well

All the trifling that dogs life's path

The special gift of the Holy Ghost

From the vantage point of heaven

Aids man in the perfecting process

As he navigates his way through life

Prepares man for every task ahead

With the divine will there to know

So he can be guided in all his labors

In noble causes that serve love well

End

Dare to Let Go

There are fears and doubts to overcome

For delay and hesitation do always attend

Before man can yield to the call of faith

And make the commitment to fully trust

He that steps forth to answer God's call

Has been marked aforetime by the divine

He will respond duly in appointed season

In gradual and progressive steps of faith

There is a battle before full commitment

In wrestling with the 'beast of Ephesus'

Tis the old which the believer has known

Battling the new he does not fully know

Dare to Let Go (Cont'd)

Tis quite a struggle to let go of the past

But the young has to be brave in faith

For the path of spiritual transformation

Is only for the lion-hearted to master

End

Humble Pulse

To seek for a rendezvous with the divine

Is to embark on a search for the Truth

And walk in footsteps of obedient faith

To where love and life reign supreme

A life of communion with the Father

Takes roots that are deeply anchored

In faith that affords man sheltered life

Where the Star of hope shines in love

To help the seeker in staying the course

Star of Hope serves as direction finder

Transmits the pulses to guide and steer

In light of truth through divine power

Humble Pulse (Cont'd)

❦

The pulses received in the light of truth

Is spiritual food that sustained Daniel

And fellow captives in courts of Babylon

As humble pulse for soul, mind and body

End

Pulses of Hope

Sacrifices made in goodness breed hope
As pulses of life in the stream of the pure
Such keeps the traveler from getting lost
Affords him the means to make it home

The noble framed in light by love and truth
Finds safe dock in the divine station above
Amid forays in light to find pasture as due
With blood of the lamb to keep death afar

Thru life's disappointments and letdowns
To plant precious seeds of hope in love
Yields a vineyard attended by the divine
To produce that which endures and fulfills

Pulses of Hope (Cont'd)

He that harvests from the divine vineyard

Is in regeneration where all can be had

For wisdom borne in light is his to have

To bring about all that his mind envisions

End

Time Makes a Demand

Time demands an accounting from man

For every gift that life bestows on him

The faith of the recipient will be tested

In trials, temptations and tribulations

Time separates the future from the past

To mold a vessel fit for each new season

But the young and faithless are misled

To attempt to patch the old on the new

The enemy of light mixes right and wrong

Tis better to watch for his devious plots

He peddles the impure and compromised

All to lead the infirm back to a dead past

End

False and Compromised

Hypocrite that has been denied same

Works to hinder men from receiving it

Key of knowledge that he truly covets

Precious gift that sets noble souls apart

Labels the pure as blundering heresy

So the young may not embrace Truth

And parades himself as an angel of light

While he aims to shield out the true

The search for truth and understanding

So man can know the will of his Creator

Ends only when God finds that heart

Large enough to receive his handprint

The hearts God touches are such that love

To aspire for truth and seek for wisdom

Whose steps are guided by the true light

And care not for the false or compromised

End

Destiny's Man

Every person of destiny is an elect one

Known from birth to be divinely chosen

Events, circumstances and experiences

Do add up to frame his life for all to see

The hearts chosen and anointed by God

Share an unmistakable common prolife

Quite a vivid and defining portrait it is

The same yesterday, today and forever

Always of a lineage from a distant past

With a celestial sign to herald their birth

And another to tell of their departure

After a brief sojourn through the earth

Destiny's Man (Cont'd)

There's a path that destiny ordains afore

For the elect by a new way not foreseen

And special purpose not fully understood

That brings the better to all in due time

Such are souls come from exalted places

As conveyors for the better from above

To model and frame immortality's face

And help lift the earthly into the starry

End

Cogs in the Divine Wheel

The sons of Light do mount up as eagles

Borne on the steps of a cosmic escalator

As cogs in the divine wheel that ever turns

From heaven down to earth and up again

Such cut a parabolic arc over humanity

So men can be uplifted with them thru light

To the womb of love and the realm of Life

Back home from whence they were sent

The sons are given to overcome the world

For goodness that uplifts is laden in them

Tis the treasure of heaven as the telekinetic

To help men rid the heaviness of darkness

Cogs in the Divine Wheel (Cont'd)

Such are ground breakers come to rebuild

The broken and wasted the bereft of hope

Through greater love that counts no cost

By power of truth and light over darkness

Cogs that can thresh mountains in the way

Are the teeth of justice for the poor as well

To set the earthly table for many without

Just as Heaven prepares and sets for them

Tis wisdom that reaches all who ask in love

In insight and keys to bedeviling problems

To guard against the onslaught of the evil

And darkness that attempts to screen light

Cogs in the Divine Wheel (Cont'd)

The sooner that man comes into light of truth

Is sooner that the shroud that drapes the land

And keeps the souls of men in a darkly veil

Is lifted off so love's flame can blaze for all

End

Matured in Grace

Grace is the safety net in the formative days of youth

When the young have weak spiritual legs to stand on

Tis vicarious living to nurture from infancy to maturity

For all willing to trust in the power of sacrificial love

It flows through spiritual nipples that the elder offers

So the young may obtain the essential and the needed

Takes grace to protect from the hidden traps and pits

Laid by wolves who prey on the lambs on faith's way

Grace is the essence that sustains in the kingdom way

A divine constant that is ever flowing for the faithful

But tis a window that closes when the feast is infected

By the false confessors who live not truly in the light

Matured in Grace (Cont'd)

The heart that sincerely desires after things divine

Is soon transformed in time into a son in good grace

As a vessel worthy to receive the sweet rain of mercy

That alights from above to delight all faithful souls

The transformed are given to wear eternity's cloak

As points of light in every land, culture and tongue

For such are the trees of righteousness left standing

After the unproductive are felled by the axe of time

They are given to act through the impulse of love

By certain will communicated in light of living truth

In thoughts and footsteps as imprints of the divine

To be heralds of the better availed only thru grace

End

Souls Lost in the World

The honorable partaker of grace is soon established

And duly welcomed into the peace that mercy avails

But unworthy partakers become blinded in the way

As the misguided and selfish soon turned into fools

The true wealth and fullness of the riches of God

Are the precious and cherished gifts borne thru love

Such are not for the blind wise in own eyes to possess

Nor for the souls lost for loving the world too much

The man of the world may be ample on his left hand

But he cannot please God when the right is withered

For both hands are vital to accomplish good works

Needed to wrought that pleasing and well-received

Souls Lost in the World (Cont'd)

Love of the world leads to futile and sterile works

In ostentatious endeavors aimed for praise of men

Such are clumsy attempts to hide behind the fig-leaf

Which neither affords the soul fulfillment nor peace

End

A Glimpse of the Divine

True charity embodies the essence of Christ

Same it takes to be established under mercy

In selfless acts performed as burnt sacrifices

For the benefit of all and not for self-glory

Material gifts tell not the tale of charity fully

Only a swipe at the surface and not the core

It involves time, efforts and materials least

In sacrificial love that enlightens all touched

Charity does exact real and opportunity costs

It denies the self of the things wanted in life

So that the deprived can have what is needed

Such that they cannot have any other way

A Glimpse of the Divine (Cont'd)

Charity frames faithfulness so all men can see

Not as an indication of abundance or excess

Nor statement of affluence or being well off

But in service for all in the spirit of divine love

It asks for living so that goodness can abound

And ushers in the enlightening and revelatory

For where charity is rendered and received

There man can have a glimpse of the divine

End

Heavenly Side of Earth

The mount of transfiguration is for the merciful

Heavenly side of earth that only a few ever know

Tis mountaintop where the pure dew descends

And all things stand in reflection of God's glory

Tis for those who walk in the way of the righteous

Where all who come desire to stay and not depart

Place of redeeming light where all who have been

Can eat the fig from the platter of the everlasting

With the sword of the word or bullets of thoughts

And insight into the needful from present to future

There the mind is focused to invite things sublime

To expose the wicked and the false in divining light

Heavenly Side of Earth (Cont'd)

He who stands on the mount will find divine riches

As transformed in spirit who has much to inherit

He may lose much in the interim for love of truth

But best in life awaits him on earth's heavenly side

End

Divine's Applecart

The anointed is able to receive true gifts

Golden apples served from the divine cart

Tis the wisdom able to transform thoughts

Into things that can be seen by men's eyes

The faithless misled by agents of darkness

Upsets the applecart through contention

Has neither patience nor trust in the Divine

Whose promises never fail for the faithful

The golden apples of wisdom are revealed

To faithful hearts in good and timely order

As the precious to decorate attentive ears

And used by heaven to shed glory on man

Divine's Applecart (Cont'd)

The word of truth is often times revealed

To pierce the veil of darkness in men's heart

So as to discomfort and rid the unfaithful

Of the delusion that sin can be hidden

Tis truth never revealed to mock or deride

But only to shine the light in good hope

To help the faithless see his way in the light

And find a portion of wisdom's apple as due

End

Power and Sound Mind

Man willing to forsake material gains for divine gifts

Is a candle to shine forth true light so men can see

He's one bestowed with spirit of power and the mind

That speaks in truth from the lowly to the powerful

His voice rings clearly and loudly so all can hear

To declare God's truth that is duly entrusted to him

As that herald of the last chance and ebbing hope

'fore light's last gleaming and darkness comes to call

Such that are anointed and called in righteous service

Must be strong of faith and be ready to withstand

The barrage of the fury of the agents of darkness

With bravery that quits not and vision that fails not

Power and Sound Mind (Cont'd)

Power and sound mind is for the man reborn in spirit

For the triumphant who does not give up the fight

Even where there seems to be little reason to hope

Until vestiges of darkness become brightened by Love

End

Season for Change

Tis a season appointed for the old to make way for new

When things look good without but are rotten to the core

A time that captures the peak of man's spiritual ugliness

As the grip of darkness holds many souls in deadly choke

Tis period of unparalleled hypocrisy that calls for change

As the mask of spiritual purity hides moral decadence

In a time when there are clouds of deception everywhere

Where the fake and false is chosen over the real and true

Tis a time of grand masquerade of the agents of darkness

When many such deviously pose as messengers of light

As religion proliferates in lip service and false confessions

But spiritual famine besets men's swelling congregations

Season for Change (Cont'd)

Alas the collective soul of humanity craves the material

As the appearance of spiritual revival decorates the land

In excessive consumptions that afford little satisfaction

But maroon many on the parched deserts of wantonness

Tis a time of great anguish in heaven at man's hypocrisy

When the stink of human corruption reaches the exalted

As a low point that foretells the collapse of the existing

And beginning of a pristine where nothing ugly can hide

End

Triumphant in Life

The spirit triumphant is bestowed on the anointed

On watchman with eye of the spirit focused above

Much grace flows to lead him on the righteous path

There to obtain in mercy and share with all in love

Takes grace to make mountains become mole hills

For without it problems do seem so insurmountable

Aids the faithful bestowed with a spirit triumphant

To find that pass even where the mountain is real

The triumphant has the withal to thrive in all times

For the table of goodness and mercy is set for him

As one destined to travel calmly on life's long road

With the face of Benevolence ever smiling on him

Triumphant in Life (Cont'd)

Entrusted to him is great vision and strong faith

The ladder up to the celestial such turn out to be

That soon uplifts the earthly into the heavenly

And afford man victories that are stellar to behold

Great courage and wisdom is availed through faith

So life's problems turn into a garden of promises

Laden with the seedlings of amazing opportunities

For the spirit that triumphs through all challenges

End

Way of Light

The way of light leads ultimately to a new birth

In a journey that leads certain men thru a maze

Past certain places to live through certain events

And be presented with certain choices to make

The life and teaching of Christ provide a model

For man's regeneration if followed in good faith

A never failing guide for the successful navigation

Of life's slippery slopes and precipitous terrain

Heaven's tableland is the abode of the saintly

A command for those who aim for a portion there

Embrace love and truth for therein is God found

And strive for those works that shine before all

Way of Light (Cont'd)

To be connected with the divine is a priceless gift

Although it can be very costly to the faithful

For enlightenment by truth is an uphill endeavor

But gain of eternity far outweighs the troubles

Faith calls the believer to love his fellow man

And treat all the same for it is the way of light

A good framework for divine consciousness too

And golden rule that leads to the Father's heart

End

Thankfulness is Essential

Thankfulness does pave the way in life's winding path

To keep and maintain the good in ever flowing grace

Such plants the seeds for victory on the walk of faith

And works so that life's burdens can be much eased

Thankfulness costs very little yet it can give so much

To affirm goodness that's rendered and well-received

For it refreshes the soul and revives the depleted spirit

And puts a smile in the heart wearied of life's troubles

Thankfulness reassures during down moments of life

To help man realize that he does not labor in vain

When truth falls on deaf ears amid rejecting hearts

And weariness of flesh leads footsteps to drag heavily

Thankfulness is Essential (Cont'd)

Thankfulness for the prayers answered and yet to be

Fills the faithful man with renewed hope and songs

In knowledge that God's truth does not return void

And his words of promise do eventually come to pass

Thankfulness to God for all the good things in life

And tender mercies that faithfully attend true belief

Prompts the delighted heart to sing heaven's praises

In voice tuned by grace to attest to divine goodness

The good in creation do respond in joyful harmony

When praise is rendered to God from worthy lips

Then are stiff tongues loosened so all men can join

In a feast of love that links together heaven and earth

Thankfulness is Essential (Cont'd)

In hearts and tongues where the word of God rings true

Thankful tunes to the divine Father therefrom arise

Such hearts will be shielded from the evil in the world

To see much goodness abound in and around their lot

Thankfulness for hope of eternity and the passport of Life

Frames good hope that puts a bounce in a man's steps

And allows life's soothing melodies to filter into the heart

That knows that he walks as part of love's congregation

End

Changes thru Drought

Drought or deprivation is often ordained

To play a transforming role in a man's life

Tis through the times when he is in lack

That the light of reality helps him to see

The things that are truly important in life

So he can sort his earthly lot as he should

Unimportant things do take up much room

To encumber the soul and choke the spirit

Only when such that hold back are let go

Sorted and buried as part of life's trash

Does the spirit in man spring to full life

So he can afford to have the truly fulfilling

Changes thru Drought (Cont'd)

Cessation of the rain does bring deprivation

To the faithless man as well as the faithful

Takes three years for the good to be rooted

And same for root of the ugly weed to wither

But the faithful is not much for wear thru all

For his needs are handy and are easily met

The faithful handles deprivation well enough

Knows that in any state that he finds himself

Contentment with godliness suffices for him

For he's a vessel fitted to handle life's waves

As Destiny's own ordained to be the intrepid

To come through life's hardships unscathed

Changes thru Drought (Cont'd)

❧

The rains cease so the ugly weeds can shrivel

And the good that's lovely can be attended to

With little to distract and mislead in the way

Much can be afforded by grace through faith

So that the man who endures well in droughts

Is well prepared to abound in goodness in life

End

Baptism in Fire

Deprivation does bring a baptism of fire

And for the faithful a season of change

The baptismal flame does brindle him

Yet his core is protected and untouched

Man brindled but not scorched within

Is one pruned and transformed in spirit

To produce good and enduring works

Such works that endure to shine in glory

Takes the spirit purified in fire to ascend

To the mountainous abode of the rains

Therefrom to bring spiritual dew below

As water bearer to restore the withered

Baptism in Fire (Cont'd)

Such is the soul joined up with the divine

Whose footsteps are guided to the place

Where the delightful provisions are found

And the essential to revitalize are availed

The baptized in fire is a vessel purified

One acceptable to receive heavenly gifts

As a source of comfort in troubling times

To aid weary hearts and faltering steps

End

Man is the Monument

Many choose the building of monuments

As platforms for self-glory in name of God

The accolades and praises received by such

Serve as due rewards for all their troubles

But the bearer of light is a true monument

As joint possessor of a new heaven on earth

Such do choose to forego earthly rewards

And seek after blessings of the divine first

He that loves God does not deny the Truth

But receives and keeps much for the people

What he has he holds in custody for them

As divine gifts received for the good of all

Man is the Monument (Cont'd)

The fragrant anointing is poured from above

On the monument who lives in a pure stream

Always ready and willingly to serve in faith

As the divine wills and acts in love thru him

End

The Edifice Stands

He who lives in the eternal stream is a chosen vessel

Laden with the precious and configured to endure all

He is one well prepared as an all-season utility vehicle

To weather all kinds of troubles and trials unscathed

He'll pass thru the stormy wind to prove his integrity

And the earthquake to confirm his certainty in God

At last comes a test of fire to reveal his core content

Yet he weathers all as an edifice made strong by faith

The stormy wind is the harbinger of drastic changes

And manifests as that which sorts the real from fake

Tis wind of separation to sift the wheat from the chaff

That leaves the faithless man helpless in its wake

The Edifice Stands (Cont'd)

Behold the information age descends on all as a storm

In a season of full blossom of the fruit of good and evil

To have mankind overwhelmed with much knowledge

In a service platter of both the useful and poisonous

Man harbors the shallow feeling of being empowered

In collective consciousness borne of information's feast

Yet tis a sad delusion to be empowered by the stormy

That beguiles and intoxicates many into spiritual death

Mankind cannot restrain the evil borne of the storm

As it funnels the faithless into a vortex of destruction

Where many unwary souls have been swept along

To be road-kill discarded for lack of true knowledge

End

Quake and Fire

There is a divine quake that follows the stormy

To bring down things weakened but still standing

Quakes and temblors that topple the unneeded

Things to be jettisoned that have run their course

It quakes to validate things that have deep roots

And are anchored on rock from those that aren't

Quakes to affirm all who are at peace and sway

In a rhythmic harmony with God's sovereign will

The quake brings down all such with feet of clay

That utilize size and clout to control the people

Like pebble fashioned by God and used by David

That topples Goliath the unsustainable behemoth

Quake and Fire (Cont'd)

❧

The pillars of morality have been assayed for little

And long standing institutions are primed to fail

Wealth as the answer to life is no longer credible

As the props of society have started to crumble

At long last comes truth's fining fire to determine

The souls afforded a place in the realm of the true

The sanctified in truth that have passed judgment

And worthy to receive the eternal passport 'to Life

End

In Tune with All

The anointed is never overtaken by whelming floods

For he is given to have the pertinent and prescient

Such pass through the information deluge unscathed

And receives due knowledge without the intoxication

The anointed can communicate with much in nature

For he is in tune with the divine and with all as well

As one well-informed with that needed for the day

Who is never grounded in life by fears and worries

The anointed is guided in accordance with God's will

To pass through life's temblors and not lose focus

For he's one certain that walks the strait and narrow

Who knows where he's going and never strays away

The anointed is thankful and counts all his blessings

And never throws up for he is filled with the needful

He will never be scorched as he passes thru any fire

For his spirit has been forged in a furnace of truth

End

Best and Worst

The spirit of evil masquerades as truth

To lead unwary souls into pitiful demise

But the best of humanity remains shielded

For such are saved by grace through faith

Life on earth is akin to a divine distillery

With light of truth to catalyze the process

That separates and purifies souls of men

So the purified rises but the debased falls

Pure in spirit live in a higher consciousness

Lifted up in that wise are the sons of light

As the reborn given to live above the world

In fellowship with others of kindred spirit

Best and Worst (Cont'd)

The rest of mankind have been left to sink

Into a lower pit of human consciousness

As souls that are earthy and dehumanized

Debased in spirit no better than animals

World of the carnal is left for the debased

For soulless ones who feast on each other

There's the best and the worst of mankind

With a sure firmament to keep both apart

End

Earthly and Cosmic Clocks

There is a cosmic and an earthly clock to mind
With different purposes for each clock to govern
The earthly clock ticks as man searches for a path
For a way to reconnect with his divine root in time

The path of light is way that avails man an escape
From the leash and the ravages of earthly sojourn
Into the cosmic stream that entails the everlasting
Where death's cold hands can touch him no more

Such is a universal spirit freed of earthly shackles
To belong no more with the earth but the cosmos
For he is then under an interminable cosmic clock
Able to traverse in spirit 'tween heaven and earth

Earthly and Cosmic Clocks (Cont'd)

Many are stuck on earth with no hope of escape

And remain hopelessly lost in a dark endless loop

Not able to reconnect with their divine root in time

As objects lost because they rejected the true light

Quest to find that which was lost is life's true tale

Tis fate of the blind told in saga of the prodigal son

Man that finds his way home in good earthly time

Is one that is crowned with the gifts that are eternal

Earthly time for the race and the cosmic for a prize

Man's euphoric elation at the last-second shot made

And the field goal kicked thru that says game is over

Are earthly events that hint to glory of timely escape

End

Idealizing Space and Time

Space and time keep the accounts of the book of Life

Man's availed an earthly plot to create the good there

And afforded time for his handiworks to be judged

So the lot in good order is made fruitful and multiplied

Goodness and mercy attend the path of the righteous

As complementary duo in the grand universal scheme

Both are the vehicles that delight as well as afford

The means to 'see' the face of God in space and time

Space and time are spun off from the heavenly loom

To be the framework that direct matter and energy

As those two run the errands for goodness and mercy

All by divine impulse and love of the heavenly Father

Idealizing Space and Time (Cont'd)

The gentle sweet voices of goodness and mercy

Motivate those who travel in stream of the eternal

Certain men who do certain things at certain times

As matter and energy idealized in space and time

Faithfulness always yields to God's sovereign will

So that as goodness and mercy fill the ghost of time

Man can wake up in spirit in the image of the divine

To find his earthly lot made fruitful and multiplied

End

Fire and Light

The man that has made it to the Holy Mount of God

Has passed through the baptism of the fire of truth

Tis baptism that bestows the anointing of the Spirit

And lights up man's heart with the flame of Love

He that has passed judgment brings fire and light

Fire as chariot of the spirit that brings man comfort

A conveyance for sacrifice worthy and well received

And the essence to fill mind and body with purpose

Light chases away fear in life's dreary dark times

When man is blind and prone to stumble in the way

And many perish for lack of sufficient knowledge

In misguided deeds done under the veil of darkness

Fire and Light (Cont'd)

The light idealized in darkness shows as a full moon

In truth that holds man accountable in night times

To fan the fire that burns away unproductive things

So that the new and better can be realized in life

End

Malaise of Uncertainty

A commitment to faithfulness is heaven's call

And choice of light over the darkened way too

Such is the path that life asks all men to take

So the earthly walk can be deemed righteous

Tis a recipe for spiritual malaise and ugliness

When uncertainty rules the heart of a man

And he will not truly commit his way to God

But straddles the fence as it suits his purpose

Feigned spirituality to cover man's mischiefs

Is a cloak of thin veneer that soon wears away

As the dark intentions and evil deeds of men

Are exposed in ugliness borne of uncertainty

Malaise of Uncertainty (Cont'd)

Ugliness is dark and forestalls spread of light

As the serpent in enchanting and fatal form

In a spirit of darkness masked as that of light

To detract and choke the flow of things pure

Uncertainty taints and weakens the vessel

Like a viral infection that slowly eats away

Keeps man down and not ready for service

Unable to step up when called to active duty

Spit of the serpent is in its charming words

But man of certainty baptized in fire of truth

Can afford life's anti-dote to the venomous

In power and spirit that exposes all in light

End

Power in Certainty

The power of the spirit works mightily for the certain

To bring transformative changes in every area of life

Makes the admirable to issue from the worst of men

And the brave to emerge from the cowardly of heart

Wisdom of the divine considered foolish by the world

Turns the man of many weaknesses into the virtuous

Soon transforms the erstwhile man of many foibles

'to the worthy by whom the tale of redemption is told

Same will have his requests given due consideration

And become a courier of life where death has stalked

For God does deliver as promised in the light of truth

So that all transformed can receive the gifts of Love

Power in Certainty (Cont'd)

The enemy aims to plant seeds of uncertainty in man

For divine power flows not where such is the case

The faithless and uncertain often deems himself wise

But turns out to be only a fool at the end of the day

Way of certainty demands total and full commitment

From the shadowy into the fullness of light and love

To where God calls all the faithful into due welcome

And divine power abounds fully for victorious living

End

Colossus from Trials

Power of God is best displayed for the faithful

In the troubled season when he's at his weakest

Tis then when the flesh's been emptied of pride

That the spirit has ample room to work mightily

The gate of Benevolence swings open for him

When man has offered up everything to God

And nothing more is left to give but the heart

So man can know from whence his help comes

Enduring gifts are bestowed freely but not free

For the good in life is wrought by a test of faith

Flesh and ego have to become inconsequential

Be mortified by trial for spirit to have full sway

Colossus from Trials (Cont'd)

Only way to victory is through faith's testing fire

A beast to be slain before each victory is secured

Tis by test of faith that the tree of righteousness

Is built up by rings of trial to become a Colossus

End

Certain in Faith

Certainty of faith yields uncommon wisdom

That avails man knowledge of the will of God

To afford him needed light in a sea of darkness

And give him means to walk by faith not sight

The certain of faith aims to win souls for God

As one divinely used to speak needed truth

He's a transmitter that broadcasts to the thirsty

A voice that reaches those who seek after light

The certain in faith spawns many followers

Sons and daughters from his spiritual perch

His offspring are often sundered far and wide

But are bound to him in an unbreakable bond

Certain in Faith (Cont'd)

The certain no longer worries but fully trusts

As one ever thankful for the blessings of life

For the power of God is always near at hand

To accomplish much thru him secure in love

He's a fountain of David that offers due praise

As living water that bubbles up from the heart

In truth that acknowledges divine goodness

All by certainty of faith founded on the Rock

End

Better Fusion than Fission

The body that lacks grace is devoid of the spirit of Life

For such is the dead that prods along through fission

Where the parts devour each other much like cannibalism

In a frenzy of condemnable activities that invite death

Though it may appear as a feast to the blind and unwary

Tis really the macabre dance of maggots in total delirium

Where the dying celebrate oblivious of impending doom

And neither peace nor fulfillment is availed man's soul

The body filled with grace abounds with the spirit of Life

Such is alive and springs forth through a process of fusion

As parts reach out in cross pollination to create new life

Through an uplifting and joyful feasting in a spirit of love

Better Fusion than Fission (Cont'd)

Such do abound in the spirit of love, goodness and mercy

With truth and understanding there to sustain all   within

As honey from each part fuse into sweet nectar of the new

With hand of God close to help and peace near to bless

Body that lacks grace is very evident for such cannot hide

He's the wise in his own eyes who loves not good counsel

And has difficulty giving thanks or showing appreciation

Ever on the defensive and asks not for forgiveness easily

Such is a self-righteous knave blind to his many faults

With manipulative schemes aimed to win men's approval

A loud but false confessor of faith who does good deeds

Only when an audience is there to laud him with praise

Better Fusion than Fission (Cont'd)

He's purveyor and victim of the false that poses as real

Who's not able to perceive the spiritual from the earthly

The blind and oblivious who plods on in sea of darkness

In pride that invites death and keeps Life at a distance

End

The Surreptitious

The old ways of man is surreptitious

Prideful, boastful and vain glorious

It is emblematic of the old serpent

That molts to cover itself in new skin

Such remains the same within its core

As an unchanging deceitful ugly heart

At home in the dark and subterranean

With clipped wings that cannot uplift

Purveyor of the earthy and transient

In a subterfuge that is far and below

Unlike that which endures and uplifts

Found in a safe refuge through truth

The Surreptitious (Cont'd)

The surreptitious wields an evil streak

As whims and fancies flood each day

With windy emotions that soon change

'to undercurrents that tow man down

Such prides itself in material excesses

That foster an ugly culture of thievery

Devoid of guilt and little accountability

In misappropriation that damns it all

Tis a cesspool of the worst in mankind

Where little with God means nothing

And might presumes to be the right

With wrong ever waxing in strength

The Surreptitious (Cont'd)

The dark ways of the surreptitious

Leads man back to the dark past

Tis a coffin that enthralls in darkness

To seduce many into untimely death

It fills the Father's heart with sadness

When creation is marred with ugliness

With such pretensions and hypocrisy

While the creature mocks his Creator

End

From Land of Truth

The man that has journeyed to the distant land of truth

Has laid down his life to know in the stream of the pure

He has love for all people but despises the dark old ways

In the greater love he shows and greater truth he tells

The essence of the land far away is the good and perfect

The enduring availed in light of truth to sustain and fulfill

Such is entrusted to the traveler as love's precious gifts

So he can return to plant the good seed in willing hearts

Tis by journey of truth that darkened hearts are availed

A chance to catch a glimpse of the glorious and free

Glory that boasts not but is dignified in hushed splendor

And can lift up the human spirit to dare to kiss the sky

From Land of Truth (Cont'd)

Tis glory of the dew that covers all with life and hope

Same glory of the flower that smiles to welcome the sun

Such glory that man once knew and will know once more

As that lost in the distant past is soon found thru truth

End

A Lick of the Divine

Man willing to lose all in the world for goodness and love

Will have his handiworks stand before heaven and earth

Such is an elect who'll be protected through life's travails

As a worthy emissary to bring light into darkened places

There is an elect son christened for every community

Within every race, color, country, tribe and tongue is one

Salt of the earth spread so all can have a lick of the divine

For Providence works so that men everywhere are served

Not many are willing to embrace the emissaries of light

Too much love for the world to pay heed to the higher

Not on account of neglect or oversight on Heaven's part

But due to man's refusal to believe first 'fore he can see

A Lick of the Divine (Cont'd)

The elect may not be openly acknowledged by the people

And might even think that he has failed in his calling

But through him irreversible changes come to be wrought

As the transformation for good sets in among many hearts

Many do come to know when light has risen in their midst

Man of ages woven from the cloth of their lowly Nazareth

They'll know that a noble spirit has been wrought by love

One little in the world that's exalted by the divine Father

He that shows the way is led on the road less travelled

A way that'll come to be desired and sought nevertheless

For long after the labor is done does victory show its face

In glory that's not tasted before but until the battle's done

End

Mantle of Grace

The man who is chosen to be grafted into the tree of Life

Must not underestimate what God has purposed thru him

He's to start a new branch in family tree of the everlasting

Upon which truth and love will blossom to bear good fruits

Man with spiritual mantle bestowed on him by the Father

Is touched to do the amazing from wisdom's lofty perch

He'll inspire and uplift many men to do greater works

As sons in light given to receive and pass the divine torch

Mantle focuses and protects love's flame from dying out

Diffuses hope's deeming glow so it will be easy on the eye

But love's shroud has to be maintained like all good gifts

With living truth that washes and purifies all things in light

Mantle of Grace (Cont'd)

That which shrouds the enlightened is perceived in spirit

Covers man as grace that flows through divine anointing

To make possible the sharing of love's redeeming flame

From the heart where it abounds to where it is lacking

End

The Prize is Ahead

He that seeks after intimacy with the divine

Must forget the injustice and hurts of his past

There must be no bitterness found in his heart

As it beclouds the mind to douse love's flame

To let the past go allows man to find the new

In a time and place where all can be golden

The wise leaves it all in God's righteous hand

So he can spread his wings and catch the wind

The tribulations of the past teach useful lessons

Strengthens man in way of love that forgives

For by the pain and passion endured thru faith

He comes to find way tween heaven and earth

The Prize is Ahead (Cont'd)

The man that returns to the places of his past

Remains bound and soon loses sight of the prize

But he that looks to the future begins life today

So he can receive mercy's goodness tomorrow

To such the past is dead and hold no stake at all

For his take is served in a future that's unlimited

Where great works are purposed and appointed

Onto him readied to answer destiny's timely call

Such has to keep his eyes ahead to win the prize

Where Providence waits when man seeks in truth

In the regeneration of things which seemed lost

And with golden crown of life for a race well ran

End

Power in Words

Anointed words and prescient knowledge

Used to address situations that life brings

So that the best outcome can always result

Is found thru the wisdom that God imparts

Words that change all things for the better

Can turn life's disappointments to blessings

To put back the spring in the sagging limb

And restore vision to the flagging eyesight

Tis same that duly changes water into wine

Or that proverbial lemon into lemonade

And means for light to overcome darkness

So death's grip over man can be loosed

Power in Words (Cont'd)

Man bestowed with truth to reach all men

Can break the stony heart with his words

Melt hardened minds with loving thoughts

And can find the pass thru life's mountains

He is one able to make the unbending yield

Who can change things from the inside out

To reshape the lives flattened by the world

Into vessels of honor meet for God's use

End

The Thessalonian

The doer of the marvelous before all
Such that bring God honor and glory
He's the Thessalonian and custodian
Of key words that untie life's knots

He's one purified in the mountain dew
And baptized in mist wrought in truth
Such that lives the life of the mysteries
Has only need for very little on earth

He is well on his way to a better place
With knowledge borne of certain faith
Ghost that passes through earth's night
To enlighten all who seek in his wake

End

Thankful and Humble

Humility is well-acquainted with the Divine

As the essence of life and all that's enduring

The humble will always be worthy of honor

For the Father favors and never resists such

Much is expected where much is bestowed

For life's blessings demand accountability

The humble spirit is well attended by mercy

And lives to give back in kind to all who ask

The heavenly gifts can only be received

By the humble with thankfulness to God

The proud revels in the spirit of the world

A rebel in God's eye if there ever was one

Thankful and Humble (Cont'd)

Thankfulness is ever in lips of the righteous

All who live not for self and world's praise

Such find goodness in same place as mercy

Where the fulfilling gifts await humble souls

End

Walkman in the Fullness

Walkman in fullness of the riches of Heaven

Ploughs with full yoke of the oxen of Israel

For the spirit of God is always near for him

There to lend divine might and power to aid

In time he becomes a spawn of perfection

In whom the Father's image comes alive

Just like Elisha with the mantle of grace

As he fanned Elijah's flame into a blaze

Such is one privy to the eternal and hidden

Who remains ever thankful to the Divine

The full blessing of Israel rests upon him

So grace can abound and mercy availed

Walkman in the Fullness (Cont'd)

Man that walks in such fullness is guided

Into opportunities where others see none

To receive favors when others are denied

In a new life of communion with the divine

He that has come into the fullness of Heaven

Has access to the third kept only for the sons

As one who's reborn in light to seed new life

Wherever he walks and in things he touches

End

Fullness of Israel

Tis okay to sacrifice the thirteenth for the people

So there is no unequal yoking within the flock

Twelve will suffice man to plow in love for God

For that number is fit for the fullness of Israel

The thirteenth is one too many not needed at all

Hinders the way and detracts from faith's walk

Tis the foil of the enemy used to corrupt the holy

As the oddity that aims to halt the spread of light

The enemy of light offers mankind the un-needed

To encumber the soul and serve cause of darkness

He despises the heart wherein contentment lives

The simple and orderly that serves not corruption

Fullness of Israel (Cont'd)

The enemy is embodied in a seductive temptress

As the ugly within that looks lovely on the outside

Tis a devious spirit that lures man 'to the earthen

And seeks to entrap the soul with wanton desires

Many are they with little reward for life's labors

Those filled with promise who got not due harvest

Takes separation from that which defiles the pure

For the ploughman to plant productively in Israel

End

Treasure the Soul

The man reborn in Light is the new Adam

Forewarned and prepared to thrive by faith

Such will have a temptress come into his life

To reprise Eve's role as catalyst in Eden's fall

The reborn lives by whispered divine truths

So he can take back victory in light and love

He'll know his Achilles heel and be on guard

For to die once is the good payment required

The old self dies as man seeks after the true

So he can receive new life in God's anointing

The new is appointed to have honey delights

As divine glory borne from carcass of the old

Treasure the Soul (Cont'd)

To keep the treasure of the soul undefiled

Is not to fall for allures of the sweet and easy

For the tempter offers man sinful delights

Such pleasures that are but poison of the asp

To have compassion but not lose the soul

Is wisdom's counsel for all baptized in truth

For weight of judgment falls on the unwary

Those who know the truth and will not heed

The man that has been favored in judgment

Is a standard of reference to be used by God

And must treasure his soul above the earthy

For he's become a star to guide other seekers

End

Possessor of the Key

The key of knowledge is never given

To those who honor not the precious

Tis only for the righteous before God

Who guard it well and live not for self

Tis key that leads into heart of creation

Both the seemingly mysterious in life

And the plain and unassuming things

That hide many secrets yet to be told

Tis secret of the undying in Aaron's rod

That has an everlasting bond with Life

And same which sustains the sojourner

Through adversity in life's dark passage

Possessor of the Key (Cont'd)

Tis key to unlock that lost in mist of time

And sure foundation for heaven on earth

For such that possess the key of knowledge

Have room reserved in the divine mansion

End

The True and the False

Wherever a true shepherd serves humanity

Another will rise up to make a false claim

But the latter is a wolf in sheep's clothing

That the people follow after in blindness

Whenever heaven anoints a son in the way

The people do anoint a fake for themselves

An usurper versed in the impure and dark

Whereas the true is availed in light of truth

The true one to be exalted in full measure

In accord with the Father's will and choice

Same the people will hold in a low esteem

Yet he is one willing to sacrifice all for love

Through it all the true son does not protest

For he knows that God is never deceived

And that time reveals the nature of things

To tell all that the false is far from the true

End

Power of the Cross

The cross opens the eyes of the people
To the knowledge of the pure and true
It is Life's trump card and a game changer
To lift the darkened veil off men's hearts

The cross is the cradle for man's new life
An altar of truth where the just is sacrificed
But the life given up on the altar rises again
To the amazement of those still in darkness

The crucifixion and resurrection of the just
Brings with   it an amazing transformation
The power of wickedness and grip of evil
Soon begins to wane among the   people

Power of the Cross (Cont'd)

The innocent sacrificed on altar of Truth

Is a divine gift received only through love

To give justice a new birth and life in place

Where it's been forgotten or yet unknown

End

Mirror of Indictment

Mankind is prone to reject the one justified

To be a standard of reference for judgment

For his way of living is a mirror of indictment

That brings injustice and wickedness to light

Mankind rather chooses the false and fake

A thief and robber in the ilk of Barabbas

Who regurgitates the old to take man back

To the dark past that should be forgotten

False one chosen and lauded by the people

Is a dark mirror that reflects not in true light

He's the false chosen because he validates

The ways of transgression loved by the blind

Mirror of Indictment (Cont'd)

Sure tis convenient and less discomforting

When man is not confronted by his ugliness

But it is not expedient to set his spirit free

For to know not true self is to remain bound

He that knows not his true self will remain

A poisoned fountain and a damaged pillar

Who cannot withstand when faced by evil

And can ill-afford to have the precious in life

End

Son of the Universe

The anointed one rejected by the people

Is a mirror in which those willing to look

Can regain sight and find themselves again

In better future of truth, light, love and life

He's a fount of living water and strong pillar

Who brings the truth that is inconvenient

To shine needed light on to darkened paths

So stumbling footsteps can right themselves

It takes bravery of the lion to embrace Truth

For the way of light happens to be an odyssey

That leads from the familiar into the strange

With reproach along the way to overcome

Through the winding trail and up the hill

Truth's odyssey leads to a sacrificial altar

Where the life sacrificed in love for goodness

Rises to carry on as a son of the universe

The son of the universe is one forever blessed

With the tender mercies of the divine at hand

For the life sacrificed thru the love that excels

Has a table prepared and set in the eternal

End

The Cave Dweller

A woeful plight when disorder is the order

And darkness presumes to be light of day

But there is always a light bearer anointed

Man of God despised and resented by many

Deemed the stranger with peculiar notions

But one fitted to reset the broken in order

Tis of no concern to the people in bondage

That their evil ways lead to strife and envy

And trigger the dark and devilish in man

Tis of no concern that such is filled with lust

That fills the air with a sense of foreboding

And drapes the land with a sheet of death

The Cave Dweller (Cont'd)

Man reared in darkness resists change most

A cave dweller who steps not outside the box

Whose comfort zone is a coffin devoid of life

But beyond is place of light and the refreshing

New vista that unfolds as far as eyes can see

Laden with promises and blossoms of hope

Champion of the old ways is a cave dweller

A bat without sight that hates the daylight

It takes the strange one to offer a new vision

So the unceasing sound of mourning can end

And man can finally step into a new morning

Into a future where all things possible await

End

Newfound Land

The immortal soul is a traveler in the spirit

Guided by Heaven's hand on ordained paths

Such who travel are led 'to a divine landscape

A new-found land that had not been known

The new place found is realm of the amazing

Where all is tended in light of truth and love

And nothing's ever wanted, lacking or wasted

For Providence and Benevolence there attend

Much is possible for man in the new place

With mind alert, body fit and the spirit willing

To accomplish the lovely that makes for glory

And show that man can do all things with God

End

Way of the Cross

The way of the cross does appear daunting

But it is a special platform that imparts glory

And attends well the pure of heart who's met

The divine approval and heaven's acceptance

At the heart of the cross lies the crucible

That sprinkles divinity's golden dust on man

For he that is crucified for truth rises again

As temple in which the divine makes a home

He rises to chase away vestiges of darkness

That remain hidden in the hearts of many

The entrenched ugliness that's been masked

With smoke, mirrors, bluster and bravado

Way of the Cross (Cont'd)

The reborn in light rises to show the new way

As he models a better and higher path for all

So the light of the true can reach many more

And willing hearts can come to know the divine

End

A Tapestry of Love

The anointed ones are heaven's ambassadors

Come to model the way of light for blind men

The wise in the world who know only in part

And are yet to see in the fullness of divine light

Takes the Spirit of the Father to knit together

His anointed ones into a grand glorious quilt

With thread of life spun from the fiber of truth

In a greater light borne of long suffering love

Such have risen everywhere to bring men hope

As the divine Father stitches this tapestry of love

Sons of light to embody the sun of righteousness

In spirit of true light for all times and all ages

A Tapestry of Love (Cont'd)

This worldwide web of sons to share true light

Is connected in life that pulses in truth and love

With the divine anointing as the denominator

And precious gift imparted to the pure of heart

Some hearts are anointed so many more can know

That the divine Father is ever patient and loving

As he prepares and chooses from among mankind

Those to evoke golden rays of the tapestry of Love

End

Fire of Demarcation

Many are there that flounder in the world's darkness

Takes love's unbreakable net to fish them out of there

But waiting on the seashore to broil each netted fish

Is fire of Truth that anoints man in light of new dawn

Many are called but not all can stand truth's broiling

Such are those that traverse tween sea and shoreline

Who can never be recreated in image of the divine

But given to spy the new from afar but not live in it

Creatures of the fifth day led in lesser light such are

For the sixth day's for those who've passed judgment

The chosen who sought for truth in the greater light

And found through faith by patient and suffering love

Fire of Demarcation (Cont'd)

The broiling in truth's fire baptizes on to eternal Life

And tunes man's spirit to heed well the Creator's bid

So as to pass from sea thru fire on to Promised land

As eternity's chosen given to be fruitful and multiply

End

Work of the Righteous

Man's heart has to be right for his walk to be too

For only then can his steps be guided by the divine

In the light of truth that love shines from above

To always lead him to right places at right times

The righteous is misunderstood while he's at labor

But he minds not men's scorn or seek their praise

For he will do works that all come to praise later

In harvest season when the fruits have ripened

The spirit of God always leads man to do the new

In unexpected ways not yet known by many others

The new is disparaged but appreciated in due time

But only after blind eyes have been opened to see

Work of the Righteous (Cont'd)

The better is overlooked and rejected at first sight

For it takes time to acquire the taste of the new

He that is worthy to be used for the work of glory

Seeks not praise when the work is yet in progress

Hunger for men's praise while the work is a-foot

Leads the footsteps to stray from the task at hand

For the praise of men is a strong down-current

That pulls away from the work ordained upstream

The faithful seeks not after the praise of men

But stays the course that's been divinely ordained

For there's much glory in the honey to be enjoyed

In victory after painful stings of men's reproach

End

True Confession

Profession spills easily from man's mouth

But true confession issues from the heart

When heart and tongue both come to agree

In all things and times regardless of cost

Then is the divine invited to come and stay

When the spirit and the flesh find concord

Something very rare and hard for man to do

And tongue speaks in accord with the heart

There! Is a heart where no dark recess is left

That will become a vault for divine treasure

True Confession (Cont'd)

A great light is evoked by true confession

With peace and serenity as welcome suitors

For tongue is never tied when heart agrees

In a sense of release and freedom from guilt

So man can then speak with uncommon truth

End

Bethany on to Ephraim

The believer that is on his way to Bethany

Has been chosen to see the new Dawn

His old self will die but a new will soon rise

To begin to see and know in a better light

In Bethany are bitter tears soon replaced

By life that offers the good, better and best

Tis there that gravity of death is overcome

As the flesh and Spirit are joined in Love

By ascension can man's spirit find freedom

To rise to the exalted heights of glory above

Where life abounds and death cannot hold

So he can dine in the company of the divine

Bethany onto Ephraim (Cont'd)

Death's anti-dote can be found in Bethany

And also the answers to bedeviling problems

Tis the blank sheet given to the visionary

To write a new script and begin life anew

From Bethany thru faith's walk onto Ephraim

Is the journey to separate the old from new

And lead into right hand of blessing of Israel

So the little with God can become duly grand

End

Heart of the True Confessor

True confession yields great power for man

Works to harmonize the two at war in him

To find elusive concord and common ground

Tween the old enemies of the spirit and flesh

The spirit that is free within man affords him

Divine peace that passes all understanding

The hidden truths will be revealed to such

As one fit to dine among an elect company

There is nothing new under the heavens

So declares the living and eternal truths

For all that'll ever be communicated to man

Has been inlaid as fine gold within creation

All is there for man to know when he is due

For the heart in which true confession exists

Where the flesh and the spirit fight no more

Has a sumptuous feast with wisdom to attend

The heart without blemish is well informed

As one polished to reflect the divine mind

For such is a mirror framed in perfecting love

From which nothing can be hidden for long

The heart that is joined up with the divine

As the noble that speaks in true confession

Will endure as Job and be dedicated as Noah

All in love that is as remorseful as David's

Heart of the True Confessor (Cont'd)

The true confessor intermeddles with wisdom

From there to receive life's key of knowledge

Then is nothing new for man under the heaven

But all gold to be spied and mined as needed

End

The Ghost and the Spirit

True confession is at the core of faith

Costs nothing but sacrifice of the ego

Such is the process by which the flesh

Begins to yield to the spirit in truth

True confession does get Heaven's ear

To help the laborer in God's kingdom

For where such is a staple of the heart

There the Spirit and Ghost are enabled

Holy Ghost is a carrier of information

To communicate to the mind of man

Tis the medium by which man logs on

To connect to God's all-knowing mind

The Ghost and the Spirit (Cont'd)

Holy Spirit is the motor of the divine

Tis the medium by which the faithful

Is connected to an eternal power grid

So he can be ready for duty as called

Both are needed and of much effect

For effective work in the way of Truth

The believer without the Holy Ghost

Works hard but he labors not in light

Such is work not directed by the divine

But for self-glory and the praise of men

And will not please or be well received

Above in heaven where it counts most

End

An Irreversible Gift

He that strives for mastery in life must desire

To have love and mercy attend him on the way

In manifold gifts bestowed thru divine anointing

Such that is wrought by baptism in fire of Truth

It takes spiritual fire to transform the man within

In changes wrought from an irreversible process

For man that is transformed is never the same

As one that has passed thru the valley of death

God withholds his hand for a time to suit his plan

As he gives occasion for the spirit to rise or ebb

Just like dams and locks control the flow of water

To release life's saver when needed for a purpose

An Irreversible Gift (Cont'd)

He that has been baptized in the fire of truth

Lives life as the spirit leads in well-directed steps

And must resist the tendency to return to the old

For he will be disappointed in what is left there

The glory to be found in the new life is far greater

Much more than can be availed thru the former

For the future has delightful treats to offer man

By appointments made in timely and good order

The one transformed by fire is the man within

Who's been prepared for the glorious in new Spirit

From the mediocrity and limitation of the flesh

As a spirit reborn for exalted duty in a new light

An Irreversible Gift (Cont'd)

Such will begin a quest to unwrap manifold gifts

In a lifelong odyssey of discovery and revelations

For the reality of what God has entrusted to him

Is much like a box that keeps on giving thru time

End

Gifts and Skills

Baptism in the fire of the spirit does bestow man

With ability to be in tune with all things in creation

It affords the clarity of mind that enables him to sense

The orderliness that dictates nature and place of things

Tis order that allows man to get rid of life's clutters

So he can strive and search for things that truly matter

Then will certain skills and abilities not shown before

Come to fully abound in a new stream of consciousness

Such it is that enables man to excel in life's endeavors

In hope reborn in divine light that opens new doors

So that he finds that he will begin to do the amazing

And such that seemed impossible all become possible

Gift and Skills (Cont'd)

To take stock of life's skills leads to countless blessings

And opens the eyes to the direction in which God leads

Gifts that compass and point to the new place of glory

As the composites that tell resurrection's tale in time

End

A Heavenly Perspective

Certain truths are revealed only in appointed season

To be received in spirit from place beyond the flesh

Tis knowledge received in a purer and greater light

As the wisdom that heaven divinely bestows on man

That which is divinely inspired does serve a purpose

For it affords man the light of greater understanding

As wisdom to lift to a higher plane when aspired for

To the place closer and nearer to the heart of God

Man is lifted up to acquire a heavenly perspective

So he can see much clearer and envision the better

And have his ear tuned to hear the voice of the divine

That informs man's spirit in tweets of the Holy Ghost

A Heavenly Perspective (Cont'd)

The whispers into the heart are but good affirmation

That assure and endue mankind with due knowledge

So man can be well prepared to deal with challenges

And handle them as mere ripples in the stream of life

End

Embryos of the Divine

The anointed word of God is Spirit

That springs to life in the due season

In such hearts where there is room

For it to be received and nourished

Tis same as transferring the seeds

Of the Divine-One into mortal man

So an embryo can develop and grow

'to adulthood in the passage of time

With faithfulness and diligent care

Adult within is the same Divine-One

A spawn in the similitude of parent

From truth's seed sown in the heart

Embryos of the Divine (Cont'd)

Man with a Divine-One within him

Shines forth as light so all can see

And lives for the cause of goodness

With mercy as his life's calling card

End

Higher and Greater

He that has received the gift of perception lives

According to a higher law and a greater purpose

Such is called to live in truth and light at all times

So that his spirit can remain ever ready to soar

Perception looks forward and never backwards

For the future gleams with the smile of renewal

But rear view of life often has tearful tales to tell

In sad echoes of the accusatory and recriminatory

Man that has the gift of perception is one set apart

Though misunderstood and vilified by blind masses

Yet he lives to serve humanity's cause in goodness

For he knows well that the future will vindicate him

Higher and Greater (Cont'd)

From place of goodwill and informed knowledge

The perceptive knows and speaks for welfare of all

As one rejected by many but embraced by the few

Who aspire for the greater and the fulfilling in life

End

Fulfillment in Godliness

The faithless who has rejected light's refining way

Will not find fulfillment on the lesser paths of life

The best that he can obtain there is the material

As shortcomings of life which disappoint at the end

Earthly acquisitions often turn out to be fool's gold

Though mistaken to be coronation by the misguided

But true contentment is never found in possessions

For the inanimate lack in spirit with little life to give

To be seemingly rich in the world but be dispossessed

Of life's true wealth to be found in the everlasting

Leaves only contention and emptiness of wantonness

When the foolish reject the fulfillment of godliness

End

The Climb

Many men answer the call to come up faith's summit

Such make valiant efforts but often end up on the ledge

A rest stop two-thirds of the way up in the long climb

That's a place of good hope but not heaven's table-land

Encumbered with issues of the flesh and worldly cares

Many reach that ledge to camp out and go no further

Such fall short of reaching the top for fear and doubt

For presuming that will or bluster trump total sacrifice

There are a chosen few willing to let go of every thing

And count not the cost so they can make it to the top

Such are the ones bestowed with full divine anointing

The numbered who join the congregation at the summit

The Climb (Cont'd)

It takes a commitment and dedication to make the climb

Tis not for everyone but those called by the spirit of Love

Such will come to know the hidden truths and mysteries

As those chosen for everlasting habitation with the Father

End

To Live by Faith

Spirit of the world is a lie that disguises itself as truth

A carnival that attempts to set the inner man at naught

Many join the charade as they see others in the parade

And crave the damning 'stead of seeking the redeeming

Most men never take the first plunge to break the law

But will follow suit when they see others transgress

For they follow the tendency of men to join the crowd

And seek safety in numbers by heading as the herd does

The enemy exploits this tendency and uses lost souls

To initiate that first act of disobedience or trespass

Then it becomes easier for others to plunge in as well

For it is mankind's folly to live by sight and not by faith

To Live by Faith (Cont'd)

Same ploy used by the enemy in Eden is at work today

To beguile and mislead the unwary to spiritual demise

Takes path less travelled to overcome such wickedness

A lesson worth learning for man's true transformation

Tis the turning point from where the work of darkness

Begins to be counteracted so light can have full sway

As man learns to say no to crowds and live by faith

For only then can he walk on the path of glory divine

End

The Corner Stones

The sons of light are corner stones of the kingdom

Ordained to bring about the new heaven on earth

Faithful stones that have been baptized in truth

In a mosaic of colors to pave and enlighten the way

With ears of the hearts tuned to hear the Divine

These sons of the righteous way are wrought in love

And well-equipped in spirit to lend helping hands

To those not matured and struggling in way of light

The cornerstones form a collective spiritual guild

That whispers words of soothing comfort into hearts

And extend encouragement to all weary sojourners

In affection that tells well the story of abiding love

The Corner Stones (Cont'd)

These sentinels join up in spirit with the angelic hosts

To commend those who are yet to finish the race

As saintly souls that serve Love's train with gladness

To sustain the sons of hope in the faith of the fathers

The train of love winds merrily along the upward way

Filled with joy that resounds in the welcoming hearts

Of thankful souls that escaped when others did not

All by encouraging love in the wake of a divine breeze

End

Bond of Love

There is a bond of love that never gives up

A precious gift found only thru faithfulness

Tis unbreakable and can never be severed

Either in heaven above or on earth below

Tis bond of love that binds all saintly spirits

Who have already finished the good race

To lead them to seek the up-and-coming

And help such finish life's race in victory

Tis love that ascertains that the sojourner

Is neither stuck nor stranded in the way

When morn's about to bid night farewell

And the glorious prize is within good sight

Bond of Love (Cont'd)

The search for eternal life is through Love

Tis not about who finishes first or last

But about living to make sure that no one

Deserving is left behind or lost in the way

The saintly soul who's filled with wisdom

Empties himself for the brother without

While the one able to stand under mercy

Offers the legs to uplift the lame in grace

For saintly souls the job is only finished

When no one deserving is left on the way

For then is the good work well and done

All such ordained from foundation of time

End

The Spiritual Housetop

The noble spirits dwell on certain housetops
In little places on the edge of life's wilderness
Such vessels are chosen and prepared by God
To glimpse the Divine and feel his heartbeat

The housetop is for oracles that speak about
Things that men do and hide in their hearts
By them some come to change for the better
As they realize that nothing is hidden in light

Only the saintly that dwells on the housetop
Can foretell the unseen and coming danger
And shout warning when the dark times loom
So that the ears given to embrace can heed

The Spiritual Housetop (Cont'd)

The saintly know to lend love's guiding hand

To help rescue all those stranded in the way

Those who are not tuned to the Holy Ghost

And not able to hear from heavenly places

Stranded is the uncertain who has presumed

To love both God and world at same time

The unfaithful unable to tune out the false

And allow the Truth to take root in his heart

End

Words Come to Life

To lack not and to slack not from truth is faithfulness

For the spirit borne of the words comes to full life

When enough has been written in a welcoming heart

To link together to recount redemption's full story

Tis a story about life for the dying and a new from old

As man matures in spirit to become a regenerator

Empowered with truth that make goodness abound

In anointed words to awaken and help life spring forth

The matured in spirit is a master chef in life's kitchen

Who speaks the right words in certain circumstances

As ingredients that blend to cook up the delightful

In time and space in accordance with the divine will

Words Come to Life (Cont'd)

The word of Truth is eternal and never passes away

As the foundation on which all things stand and rest

In same wise a word established in heart never dies

But has life in-laid that waits for a cue from heaven

The word of life may rest in the faithful heart awhile

Until the appointed time for which it was destined

Then its power will show forth to amaze in due glory

To accomplish that for which it was uttered in faith

End

Little Folly

Truth is the divine mirror by which each man

Comes to know and change the self for better

In it lies the power that can free man's spirit

To enable him soar to great and starry heights

Man asks to be told the truth but will not tell it

And so it becomes estranged as each day passes

For by mistruth and falsehood in varying degrees

All men have come to follow as the world turns

Man knows that to tell lies is not right thing to do

An acquired habit come about from Eden's fall

Sadly but yet he cannot desist from telling same

To eschew that which estranges from divine spirit

Little Folly (Cont'd)

Tis like the drunkard with his innocent addiction

The seemingly little and recreational folly of life

Soon turns into a raging fire storm out of control

That burns him when and where he least expects

End

Seed of Bitterness

Man loses bits of himself with each lie he tells

He degrades himself and humanity as a whole

For by such he disrupts the divine connection

And distances himself from the Father above

The man that cannot cease from telling lies

Is infected with an evil virus in the core within

He's given way for a harmful species to invade

And to take over the landscape of his mind

Man tells lies so as to gain undue advantage

Either in the material or other worldly ways

But lying sits not right in the human psyche

So man looks for justification in order to do it

Seed of Bitterness (Cont'd)

To live by hook or crook and any other means

Where men live only on a risk and reward basis

And others matter little if one can have his way

Is a sad irony of the short lived and regrettable

For lies plant seeds of bitterness among men

And leave a dark patch lodged in their souls

But truth is the bitter but wholesome medicine

That duly heals mind, body, soul and spirit too

End

Everlasting Words

The word of God is that ever-lasting truth

Which abides forever and never passes away

Heart that gladly welcomes the eternal truths

Belongs with him who will also abide forever

Such men are eternal vessels well prepared

Planted and established by God in all lands

Fruitful trees kept through the gospel of peace

With leaves that are ever verdant and green

The leaf of the tree is good medicine for man

As word of truth spoken from the faithful heart

To bring healing to all those who can receive

Those that embrace the light and heed in faith

Everlasting Words (Cont'd)

The fruitful tree is one borne of righteousness

And well-nourished from the fountain of wisdom

By consciousness derived from the mind of God

In everlasting words out of the wellspring of life

End

Pitchers of Living Water

God's truth has reached everywhere and everyone

Been adequately preached and well-fed to humanity

Tis left for every ear to heed and all hearts to choose

As mankind enters into the season of final harvest

To expend the flesh by over-indulging in earthly lusts

Provides little relief from excessive wants and desires

And leaves no room for spirit to flourish or mature

But saddles man with cravings unable to be satisfied

His ego misleads man to bend most of God's rules

In a headlong rush into degeneracy and emptiness

To offer him only the decadence of the old and sour

With little hope for him to taste the new and better

Pitchers of Living Water (Cont'd)

Men in whom the word of life did not take deep root

Starve for 'life' on account of unbridled flesh and ego

Such have no place in the new place that light offers

As it is only for spirits filled with living water of truth

The new is for the bearers who pitch the living water

Such who are in communion with the heavenly Father

Men bestowed with the divine anointing through light

By whom goodness overflows to reach others in love

End

Rite of the Saintly

The sons are faithful vessels divinely ordained

Who have been well prepared for these times

Such are trees who have produced good fruits

And are pruned by God to produce even more

Humanity has entered the season of the real

When God plans to shed his glory on the true

In this season when dawn is about to break

Faithfulness calls the worthy to be on full guard

Tis of utmost importance in the here and now

That the sons remain dedicated and watchful

So the fruits they bear can remain undefiled

Safe from corruption by the hand of the enemy

Maturity of the spiritual fruit takes many years

May cost fame and fortune in the short-term

In order to obtain the priceless in the long run

Everlasting gifts that can never be taken away

The humble who is willing to receive and yield

To divine will as the sovereign guide of his life

In time becomes a noble one exalted in spirit

To become a depository of the sacred and veiled

Such are the lion-hearted who have been willing

To let the old die for cause of goodness and love

As the rite of knighthood to establish the mortal

Through peace and compassion into immortality

End

Morning Appointed for Truth

The hidden truths are not understood in one helping

But are progressively revealed in the passage of time

As greater light of understanding comes to bear in life

When a believer grows and matures in the inner man

There are some truths that can never be understood

Until the season divinely appointed for them arrives

There are like seeds that remain in prolonged burial

In the good fertilized soil until the dew of heaven falls

There is a morning appointed for each hidden truth

That has to dawn before its fullness can be understood

And with mankind in the last days of this far gone age

Much has been availed for the true seekers to know

Morning Appointed for Truth (Cont'd)

God has bestowed the faithful with due knowledge

Of the hidden which constitute the meat of the word

Such for only the matured in spirit to comprehend

As keys to help man understand the mystifying in life

End

Made Possible with God

There are sons of Heaven and then the brides also

Just as there are the Colossians and the Ephesians

It has to do with spiritual maturation and capacity

For divine love is same but the ability to receive is not

The faithful with a welcoming heart for word of truth

Is a bride of the son that ministers the word in faith

The brides have knowledge of the spirit and the word

But have no knowledge of Heaven's secret and hidden

The secret things are for the sons ordained in light

Who have knowledge of the spirit, word and Father

Such have grown from brides to be fully transformed

As the chosen called very close to the Divine heart

Made Possible with God (Cont'd)

Matured in faith and heirs of the kingdom of light

Both the brides and sons serve God in distinct ways

Brides serve in good faith but with less understanding

Whereas sons serve in full and greater understanding

The best of the divine riches are reserved for last

For the sons and brides who serve faith in true love

As vessels of hope thru whom God does the amazing

To make much possible in a world become impossible

End

Best Saved for Last

When the guests are drunk with the less

Then is the best reserved served for last

Such is the wine with sweetness unknown

Served when brides are joined with sons

The best is served to those who kept faith

Ones whose eyes are rested above in hope

For those who tarried to finish the race

Through patient love that's divinely evoked

Tis for the long sufferers who have waited

To be duly suited up with eternity's cloak

For it takes that which never waxes old

To hold the new and sweet saved for last

Best Saved for Last (Cont'd)

The fullness of riches of God is reserved

For those who are commended into light

Hearts that yielded so truth can reach out

And cover them in fabric of Love and Life

The precious gifts entrusted from heaven

Are for only the noble-hearted to receive

Those who love truth and are ever willing

To forsake all if need be for Love's sake

Such find ready welcome 'to immortality

And find joy in the fulfillment of purpose

As vessels filled with essence of goodness

To share the rare delights of Benevolence

End

A Man Comes Forth

The son steps forth to be duly declared

When he has grown to maturity in time

One that is declared to have come alive

Is new reborn in love thru light of truth

Man that steps out is divinely anointed

And heavenly ordained in same order

As all that have come and gone before

As in the past, so today and also forever

The anointed first descends from above

To be seen with 'eye' of the inner-man

That seen in light is the seed of promise

An embryo planted in heart of the 'seer'

A Man Comes Forth (Cont'd)

It takes many years of faithful obedience

Seventeen rings for the tree to stand firm

In love for God and man in light of truth

To nurture the good seed to full maturity

The seed of promise grown to full term

Is the anointed declared to come alive

He's not known by words that so declare

But shines thru in a new way of life to all

The light that shines to be perceived by all

Is a sign to tell when man belongs to God

A tale that only Heaven and sons can tell

When man's anointed and borne of Divine

End

From Same Womb

The Father's glory reflects on all that he draws near

Though he remains unseen with the eyes of men

For close to his heart is the place without darkness

Where all who come into are commended into light

The commended are conformed by love and truth

To stumble no longer but to walk in fullness of light

In a stream of consciousness evoked from above

And divine touch that adds light to their endeavors

Such are like points of light in a world of darkness

Embalmed in truths within that covers them without

Same it is that sanctifies and protects man from evil

From wickedness that seeks to mar all things good

All who come to the place close to the Father's heart

Will have the divine magnetism duly induced in them

Tis the touch of Midas that purifies the base into gold

Magnetism that turns sinful men into vessels of glory

There is a magnetism when TRUTH is imparted in love

To draw men to the Father and source of all goodness

Tis impulse that is the gain of belief and loss of doubt

A precious gift that affirms the bond of Love with Life

Tis impulse that leads back to the home once known

For all who come to know the Father and his sons

Were once known by them and are spiritual kindred

Vessels of same mold come forth out of same womb

End

Power in Truth

Man can never be able to redeem himself

For his spirit is very much like a battery dead

But the dead in spirit can find new life again

By the mystery of grace when well-received

Redemption and salvation await thru faith

By embrace of truth borne of noble sacrifice

Much like a good battery recharges another

So can God's truth revitalize the dead spirit

Truth is to be well received regardless of cost

For he that does not remains a bound soul

Never to know that power which sets free

And can transform the mortal to immortal

Power in Truth (Cont'd)

The love of truth is not for the faint-hearted

But for the brave of heart able to endure all

For the world has little love for way of Truth

That asks man to take heavenly steps on earth

Much despise for the way of truth is a given

Until man can see in newer and better light

For that which makes brave the faint-hearted

Same it is that also perfects man through love

Truth expects all men to be willing and ready

To be able to endure much in the short-term

And count the greater for gain at the day's end

For Truth crowns all suitors with timely victory

End

God over the World

He that desires to see in the better light

Must be brave and reject the world's way

For it is path of the faithless that enthralls

And beguiles man into throes of darkness

He that lives in the world to revel in it

Is a lost one who plods along in darkness

Such has no desire for truth, light and Life

And will always be a stranger to the divine

The sublime is by knowledge of the divine

Availed to all who speak and live in truth

But the souls that hate truth are denied

Such goodness that's afforded only in light

God over the World (Cont'd)

The way of God and those of the world

Are truly the opposites that cannot mix

There's no place to sit on the fence in faith

For man has to choose one way or other

Love of God leads to a new life in spirit

Into the hope of eternal life in the divine

But the love of the world leads to demise

'to spiritual death and damnation of soul

The faithless that remain lost in the world

Have made an unwise and losing choice

And so must find escape in the time left

Before the earthly sojourn runs its course

End

Little and Blessed

The sons live to serve humanity in love and truth

Tis why Heaven cannot help but love them so

In endearing ways that far surpass any or such

That man has known and will ever know on earth

The son may seem little in the eyes of the world

As he has been pruned to bear fruits abundantly

But he's beloved and dear to the heavenly Father

Who hears his requests and grants them as due

Little is much indeed when God's hand is on man

For the power to do the amazing shows forth then

As goodness and the tender mercies from above

Alight as companions through life's winding trail

Little and Blessed (Cont'd)

The faithful man must listen at his weak moments

For help has been promised him and is very near

He must keep the trust during miserable times

And hold on in dark periods for light to re-appear

The hand of God is most visible in times of despair

In moments of fiery trials in the life of the faithful

Tis then that the voice of hope is heard loudest

And the power of love divine comes to delight man

End

The race for eternity is run through love

Tis not about finishing first or being last

But finishing together and making sure

That no deserving soul is left in the way

Kalu Onwuka is a prolific author who writes about faith walk in this new age of man's spiritual awareness. His books offer tit-bits on how to find a balance between the earthly and heavenly. He is a man of many accomplishments and draws his inspirational insights from many areas of life's experiences. The perceptive reader will find his books to be quite interesting and very enriching. He is a *Teacher, Poet, Lyricist, Electrical Engineer and Entrepreneur.* He lives with his wife in Southern California and they have five children

He is the author of the *On the Golden Strand* series which are discourses that encapsulate his spiritual experiences on the journey of spiritual transformation. These include The *Nuggets of Resurrection, Pulses of the Divine Heart, Etching for the Faithful Heart, No Hurry to Horeb* and other books in the work. He is also the author of the *Poems in Faithfulness to the Divine* Series which are books of poetry and songs. These include *Anthems in the Glorious Dawn, In Enchantment of Eternity, Tones of the Stellar Capsules of Divine Splendor*, and other books on the way.

www.ingramcontent.com/pod-product-compliance
Lightning Source LLC
Chambersburg PA
CBHW072018060426
42446CB00044B/2797